جولة في عالم الفن الإسلامي

Journey through Islamic Art

Na'ima bint Robert & Diana Mayo

Touch the arrow with TalkingPEN to start

→ Start   □ Info   ○ English   ○ Language

MANTRA
LINGUA

سمعتُ قصصاً عن مدينتَي سمرقند وبغداد،
وعن المُغول في الهند والمسلمين في اسبانيا.

I heard tales about the cities of Samarkand and Baghdad,
About the Moghuls in India and the Moors in Spain.

جمعتُ في يدَيَّ خيوط التاريخ الحريرية،

وبها نَسَجَ فكري رداءً طائراً :

رداء حلّق بي في رحلة مذهلة حول فن العالم الإسلامي .

I gathered silken threads of history in my hands and,
With them, my mind wove a flying cloak:
A cloak that took me on an amazing voyage
Through the art of the Islamic world.

حلّق بي ردائي إلى مدينة بغداد القديمة،
بلد المساجد، الحمّامات العامة،
حَلَبات السِباق والسُرادُق.

My cloak took me to the old city of Baghdad,
Home to mosques, public baths,
racetracks, and pavilions.

بلد القلاع الصحراوية الحصينة،
ذات الجدران المزينة بالرسوم من الأرض إلى السقف.
و فيها أكبر مساجد العالم المُسَمّى سامراء،
وتصوّرتُ أذان الصلاة وصلني منه خلال الغيوم.

Home to fortified desert castles,
Adorned with wall-paintings from floor to ceiling.
The largest mosque in the world called Samarra its home,
I imagined that the call to prayer reached me in the clouds.

حلّق بي ردائي إلى اسبانيا الْإسلامية،
حَيْثُ التقى الشرق بالغرب.
استعرضتُ العلماء،
المخترعين وكذلك الفَلَكِيِّين في البلاط،
يختبرون مَدَى المعرفة الْإنسانيّة.

My cloak took me to Muslim Spain,
Where the East met the West.
I passed scientists, inventors and court astronomers,
Testing the limits of human knowledge.

وهناك تجوّلتُ حول فَناءات مزخرفة،

نافورات من عهود ماضية وحدائق عَطِرَة.

There, I wandered through ornamental courtyards,
Past fountains and scented gardens.

انصهر تراث الفن الإسلامي
والإسباني معاً
لِيُقدّم ابداعاً تَحَقَّق في
قصر الحمراء ومسجد
قرطبة العظيم.
حَيْثُ حَيّت القِباب
والقناطر والفُسَيْفُساء
عَيْنيَّ المُتَلَفّهَتَيْن.

The artistic heritage of
Islam and Spain
Fused to create the
Al Hambra palace and
the great mosque of
Cordoba.
Domes, mosaics and
archways greeted my
eager eyes.

حلّق بي ردائي الى

الى تركيا السلجوقِيّة،

حَيْثُ تُزَيّن الأخشاب المنحوتة

المُزَخْرَفة الأبواب والمحاريب.

حَيْثُ وصل فَنّ تَصْفيف القرميد إلى درجة الكمال

وتُغطّي السجاجيد البرّاقة أرض المساجد.

أعجَبني نَسيجها شعرتُ به تَحتَ أصابعي.

My cloak took me to Seljuk Turkey,
Where ornate woodcarvings graced doors and pulpits.
The art of setting tiles reached near perfection
And bright woven carpets covered the mosques' floors.
I fancied I felt their textures beneath my fingers.

حَلّق بي ردائي

إلى سَمَرْقَنْد بَلد تيمور "الأعرج"

حَيْثُ اجتمع الحِرَفِيّون المَهَرة من أنحاء العالم.

My cloak took me to the Samarkand
of Timur 'the Lame'
Where artisans from around the
world were gathered.

البنّاؤون من الهند،
والخطّاطون من فارس،

Stonemasons from India,
calligraphers from Persia,

صاغةُ الفضّة من تركيا
ونسّاجو الحرير من دمشق.

Silversmiths from Turkey and
silk-weavers from Damascus.

أعيدوا جميعهم كأسرى لِيُجَمِّلوا مدينته،
بينما كان قصره خَيمة - كان بَدَوِّياً الى النهاية.

All brought back as captives, to beautify his city,
While his palace was a tent – a nomad to the end.

حلّق بي ردائي الى شوارع أكرا،
حَيْثُ الْإشاعات حول تاج محل تَملأ الأسواق الْمُزدحمة.

My cloak took me to the streets of Agra,
Where rumours of the Taj Mahal filled buzzing bazaars.

إنّها بِناية أقيمت تحقيقاً لِوَعْد على فِراش الموت،
رخام ابيض رداؤها
متألّقة في الضوء.

A building born from a deathbed promise,
Its garment of white marble
Shimmered in the light.

المشرق

كتابة مخطوطة من القرآن،

زخرفة عربية للأزهار وتصاميم هندسية

كلّها متناسقة

وسمّاها الشعراء "وجه الفجر المشرق".

رَجوتُ أن يضيف جمالها نعمة للأحياء

وليس لِيُكَفِّن الموتى.

صباح الفجر

Calligraphic inscriptions from the Qur'aan,
Floral arabesques and geometric designs
all harmonised
And the poets named her 'Dawn's bright face'.
I wished its beauty could grace the living
and not enshroud the dead.

كانت هذه الرحلة حُلماً، خيال طفلٍ،

غير أن كلّ أماكنها حقيقيّة.

أرجو أن يُنسَجَ رداؤك بهذه القصة

وأن تذهب أنت أيضاً الى هناك.

This voyage was a dream – a child's fantasy,
Though all its destinations are true.
I hope that your cloak will be spun by this tale
And that you will go there too.

Here are some explanations to help you enjoy the story:

Samarra
In the 9th century, after the foundation of Baghdad, the Caliph (ruler) moved his capital to the splendid city of Samarra. The Great Mosque was once the largest mosque in the Islamic world and rises to a height of 52 meters.

Islamic Spain was established in the 8th century by Muslims from North Africa who were known as Moors. For over three hundred years, Muslims, Christians and Jews lived together in a Golden Age when learning, art and culture flourished.

Seljuk Turkey was one of the eras in Islamic history. The Seljuks were Muslim rulers who took control of Persia and Turkey. Seljuk Turkey became the centre of excellence in weaving, ceramic painting and wood carving.

Born in the 14th century, **Timur 'the Lame'**, also known as Tamerlane, was a fierce and determined Mongol warrior who loved art. Whenever his armies invaded foreign cities, he would take care to protect the artisans and take them back to beautify his city, Samarkand.

The **Taj Mahal** was a monument built by the Mughal Emperor Shah Jahan in 1631 as a tribute to his loving wife Mumtaz Mahal. Legend says that she made him promise to build her a mausoleum more beautiful than any the world had ever seen.

Arabesque is an art form originally from Asia Minor. It was later adapted by Muslim artisans into a highly formalised form of intertwined flowers and plants.

The Qur'aan, the Muslim holy book, was revealed to the Prophet Muhammad (pbuh) by the Angel Gabriel. Its verses are often inscribed in beautiful patterns by calligraphers.

First published in 2005 by Mantra Lingua Ltd.
Global House, 303 Ballards Lane, London N12 8NP
www.mantralingua.com

A CIP record for this book is available from the British Library